Offcumdens

Bob Hamilton and Emma Storr

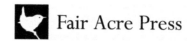

Published by Fair Acre Press
www.fairacrepress.co.uk

Photographs © Bob Hamilton 2022
Poetry © Emma Storr 2022

A CIP catalogue record of this book is available from the British Library

Paperback ISBN 978-1-911048-67-1

Cover by Bob Hamilton
Typesetting by Nadia Kingsley

Introduction

We can't agree on who came up with the title for this collection. It probably arose between us, popping up in conversation until we both realised it was right. As offcumdens, originally brought up on different sides of the Thames in London, this is our very personal take on Yorkshire, the county we've adopted as our own, even if Yorkshire will never fully reciprocate.

There is no attempt here to provide a definitive picture of the county through our words and images. It's an eclectic mix that has evolved from our individual experiences as well as from visiting places of mutual significance. We met first at a poetry event held at The Leeds Library, one of those moments of serendipity that occurred often during our subsequent collaboration. An appreciation of each other's work soon emerged and a realisation that our respective photographs and poems might combine to complement each other.

The process of pairing poems with photographs has worked in both directions, usually the poem being written in response to one of the photographs, but photographs also being matched to poems. Occasionally, both have arisen organically as a result of an expedition together to the city, coast or countryside.

The Photography

Bob: I describe myself as an opportunistic photographer. All the images presented here were taken with compact cameras, mostly with a Sony RX100, which is small enough to be slipped into the back pocket of my cycling shirts or get carried in a bum bag while I'm out running. I rarely leave the house without it.

The ready availability of a compact camera means that no opportunity is ever missed. Although this project occasionally involved searching out specific images, my photographs are usually delivered in the course of going about my everyday life, arriving randomly and unexpectedly. I love that element of surprise.

My journey as a photographer has been very much one of learning how to see, and a big part of that has been learning how to see in black and white. I can still be surprised at the result of converting a colour image to monochrome in the digital darkroom. Removing the colour helps our eyes to look deeper, to see the patterns in the image rather than simply the subject. It helps us to see below the literal surface of things, into the realm of symbol and metaphor, an evocation of something that's not in the image itself but in our own experience. A colour image is a representation. A black and white image is more akin to a poem.

The Poetry

Emma: My equivalent of Bob's compact camera is a notebook and pen, stuffed into a bag or pocket. At medical school, I wrote light verse, mainly in rhyme. Humour was a good way of dealing with the inevitable stress. When I moved to Yorkshire in the 1990s, I squeezed in a few creative writing classes while working as a GP, medical educator and mother. The experience of sharing work and discussing it in a small class was invaluable. During my MPhil in Writing at the University of South Wales, I began compiling a series of poems based on my experiences of working as a GP and of being a patient myself. This became the pamphlet, *Heart Murmur* (Calder Valley Poetry, 2019).

My poetry is still evolving. It's an exciting and unpredictable process, often surprising me in much the same way that Bob describes when looking at his photographs. Writing is a way of tapping into the unconscious river swirling below the surface, as liable to flood as to dry up. It can also emerge at unexpected places.

It's important to me that my writing is accessible and enjoyable. To choose the right words for the few lines of a poem is hard work. All the poems in Offcumdens have gone through multiple iterations. Sometimes I find the discipline of writing in a particular poetic form proves helpful. Perhaps that is why, besides free verse and concrete poems, you will find Japanese haiku and a tanka, three sonnets and a pantoum in this collection.

Contents

Offcumden

A Yorkshire term typically used to describe someone who was not born in the county

I didn't know I'd fall in love with bleak:
the swerve of dry stone walls around the hills,
the fissured scars of rock above the fields.

I'd never found an ammonite before
one nudged its corrugations out of mud
and curled its spiral shell in my palm.

I'd never heard of words like wapentake,
or village names that twisted lips and tongue:
Yockenthwaite and Muker, Thorpe and Keld.

I didn't know I'd leave the swarming south
for winter dark and outstretched summer days
to trace my Viking name on Whitby graves.

Mirror

I'm walking in sky. I'm diving in clouds.
Above my head are floating leaves,
a bench for lovers wrapped in
each other who watch their
twins share a kiss
in the black
water.
White
crepuscular
rays stream light,
a backdrop to this henge
of trees, poised by the tarn, each
branch and twig a repeated rhyme.
I'm diving in clouds. I'm walking in sky.

The Leeds Library

I can't remember when a searching hand
stopped to touch my covers, run a finger
down my spine embossed with golden letters.
Stories stay within my brittle pages,
my chapters filled with worlds no-one explores.
I have no eyes, no ears to hear the words,
but in my paper heart I long for Jane
to lift me down, release my printed voice
from dust and dark. I'm indexed, stamped and shelved
with other tomes. I haven't moved in years.
My vellum neighbours keep me shut, upright.
When footsteps on the spiral stairs approach,
the metal walkway quivers and I hope
to be retrieved, removed and browsed, chosen.

Busker

She pulls the bow across the strings
and resonates. The sound is deep
within her body, heart and gut
in harmony with notes that float
along the street, sustained and clear.

The shoppers hear a thread of sound
grow and widen into chords.
They turn and catch a snapshot glance
of beautiful: her poise and skill,
the flow of music out of wood.

Wall

The grass bends in the wind on either side
and I'm not certain what this wall keeps in,
or out, as sheep traverse its cripple holes
to graze the fields surrounding Crackpot Hall.
I wonder at its age and how men chose
the interlocking rocks with throughs and ties
to curve it high and bold towards the ridge,
a solid ripple in the outspread land.
Thin rain falls and loosens roots and edges.
The wall resists, holds back scree and slipping
slopes of gritstone skirts, spread below the scar.
The wall remains, pebbles wedged in its heart.
It clings onto the dipping, rising dale,
stretches up a glacial contoured trail.

St Aidan's, RSPB

The twitchers perch and wait and count,
identify the silhouette
that doesn't fit: a crested grebe
among the screeching mob of gulls.

No-one talks. We watch them watching.
It's not clear how this trio met
or if they're strangers on the bench,
sharing in a silent vigil.

Ears tuned, binoculars in hand,
they untangle the mingled calls,
and listen for the bittern's boom,
the kleep-kleep of the avocet.

They track the terns' erratic flight
above wild swimmers' hooded heads,
while godwits pick their way through reeds
as if on slim stiletto heels.

And keeping guard on Oddball's frame
a falcon sits, surveys the site.
The birders tick their lists and take
a flightless path from bench to car.

Letter to Prof Armitage

Dear Simon

I'm writing out of angry desperation.
Where is that hidden seventh Stanza Stone?
I've searched throughout the moors for its location.

I climbed Pule Hill with poles and booted feet,
descended to the quarry to read *Snow*,
consumed a sandwich on the Poetry Seat.

Next I found your horizontal *Rain*,
letters carved in gold across the rock,
chiselled words that rippled through the grain.

Mist proved hard to find in stormy weather.
I stumbled in the gusts on Nab Hill's crest,
spied the twin stones sheltered in the heather.

On I trudged towards the gateway where
the riven gritstone *Dew* was green with moss.
A downpour soaked my clothes and tangled hair.

Near Ilkley my wet boots became wetter.
The *Puddle* stones were lying flat in peat,
raindrops gathered in each runnelled letter.

Drenched, your poem *Beck* stood in a flood
from ghylls and gullies draining off the moor,
the words half-hidden under gorse and mud.

Six is good but seven was your remit.
Is it resting in your poet's shed,
waiting for a tweak and final edit?

Or is the seventh stone the Holy Grail,
elusive to the last? I want to know
why it's missing from the Stanza Trail.

Please email, text or phone me when you can.
You may be busy but I'd like an answer.
Yours truly, Emma Storr, frustrated fan.

Dancing Girls

Sticks are weapons in the fight
to keep going, trolleys dragged
along like stubborn kids.
They sit and chat with their hands
signing across the traffic noise,
laugh at puns spun on fingers.

Margaret insists on her full name.
Not Meg or Maggie. Else teases,
spells out Maggot, meticulously.
Rose recalls their many sweethearts,
the spilling miles of cloth each day
wrapping the world in Saltaire yarn.

Sometimes they slip out of frame,
leave stiff joints in a heap.
They run to the mill and find their clogs,
dance and stamp on sandstone floors,
feel the beat vibrating through
their tuned bodies, deafened ears.

They weave and twirl, moist with heat,
until it's time to clock off,
shuffle back to old age.
Else is sad, Margaret cross,
Rose pretends she doesn't mind
wide-fitting shoes without a heel.

Cycle

At home you don't change
out of your spattered Lycra.
First, you wipe mud off my frame,
clean the narrow space where the brake wire
rests on my lightweight scaffold.
You detach my pedals,
cradle them in your hands
before they are plunged in hot water,
soaked and cleansed.

My chain is caked with Yorkshire soil.
You brush it off from the links,
from each sprocket.
You spin my wheels in soft damp cloths
removing grit and dirt
caught in the treads.

You trickle oil onto my cogs
and leave me shining,
drying in the evening light.

Next day I return your affection:
our bodies united as
we scale the hills together,
synchronised in effort.

Breathless at the tops
we survey hay meadows
sprinkled with barns
before we descend,
freewheeling
in a whip of wind
home.

Huggate Poetry Bench

We're enfolded in the Wolds Way,
embraced by green, the shock of dry valleys.

Cows face east, graze along the creased slopes,
we sit and rest against a curve of words.

I write a poem to dips and shadows, the creep
of woods, a furrowed field of chalk and flint.

I speak my couplets to the cattle, wait
to see if they look up. They ruminate,

defecate, and make their verdict clear.
You comfort me with chocolate, a kiss.

Legend

Clumsy, clumping Rombald heaved his giant feet
through the valley, scattering boulders as he fled.

His wife pursued, chose her missiles carefully,
gathered them to hurtle, wound, spilt stone circles

from her skirts to slow his hopeless, helpless flight.
His stomp-stamp cleaved the rock. Separated Cow

from Calf. They stand confined in peat and bracken,
bellowing with the wind, eroding in the rain.

Cinematic

Past the pillars, kiosk and through the doors
we walk into Edwardian: varnished wood,
gas lamps, plush red carpet on the stairs,
folding velvet seats in obedient rows.

I follow the painted gold finger pointing
to the Ladies, just to admire the brass
handles, locks, ceramic chain pull,
the solid wooden throne, warm and wide.

The Pullman chairs embrace us. We relax,
lick ice cream from wooden spoons.

The film starts. Not a silent movie.
Capernaum is a 21st-century epic:
street children in Beirut, hungry
and hunted refugees, a toddler

in the care of twelve-year-old Zain.
No one warned me. My pockets
empty, I weep into my scarf. A lot.
Afterwards, we leave without talking.

I think of how we nestled down
into the safe cushioned seats,
while everyday life in Lebanon
walked naked across the screen.

Upright Motives

Mick knows all the curves,
the corners where moss can lurk.
He tickles out dirt.

We admire his art,
his steady stroke of wet brush.
The Glenkiln Cross gleams.

I spot a poet,
hear his voice of black treacle.
We share names and words.

Under bronze totems
Mick is map, catalogue, guide.
You take his portrait.

We leave the sculptures
floodlit in autumn sunshine.
The morning opens.

Dog Days

Mabel belongs to me. I walk her daily,
attached, so she doesn't stray, lose herself.

The streets are busy. I keep her close past shops
where friendly waves and words greet her.

She likes that. Our house is dark and empty
now there's only us. We sleep downstairs.

We take our time to cross the market square,
the lumpy kerb and scattered pavement.

We stop, often. She rests, lights up. I know
her favourite spots to sit along our route.

She mutters to me, mithers on about the rain,
the cold, her legs and whether Pat will call.

I don't reply until I've had enough:
I growl at her, pulling on her lead.

Obedient, she turns for home. We shake
our coats, feed and lie down on the rug.

Brocken Spectre

Scattered sun lends
> your shadow stilts.
At your feet, the moor
> is scored with paths,
ancient traces from
> the wakes of ships
steering through the ice
> and heathered peat.

Around your head
> a halo of light,
glinting on the cliffs
> of sandstone grit.
Seconds later you have
> disappeared,
swallowed in the tide
> of rising fog.

Grand Départ – Côte de Cray

A surge of wheels, piston limbs and taut bums
power past in silence, swathed in cheers.

The crowd leans in, cameras primed to snap
the blur of heroes in the slipstream's flow.

Lycra legs. Insect heads. They ride as one
enormous beast: a swaying, throbbing pulse.

A gust of heat blows through and then they're gone.
The peloton moves on devouring miles.

Eighteen miles

of cloth a day would stretch from
        Shipley to Skipton.

Our worsted's as soft as clouds
        or a breeze on water.

Sometimes I hum in time
        with the shuttle's flight.

I can't hear the tune but the notes
        get caught in the warp.

The Master would smile to know
        his hanks of weave

had music as well as pattern
        in every thread,

the song of my loom like a hymn
        in his sandstone church.

Exposure

He prefers fog,
the way it holds the trees
in grey aspic, leaves
their trunks glistening.

He runs up the moor
past cup-and-ring graffiti
scored in the millstone grit.
He has to be quick

to catch those winter arms
grasping the air,
larches looming
out of the gloom.

His shutter-frame eye
lines up the shot,
a black and white wink
before the morning

sharpens edges,
firs resume their
sentry duty and day
puts on her green coat.

Shelter

Grounded in Shipley
they count snowflakes,
hope this shelter is a Tardis
about to fly them out
of the damp, dank air
to somewhere, anywhere
warm, dry and green
in another galaxy.

Landed in Shipley
cooling fast, they dread
taking cold hands
out of soggy gloves to text,
check bus cancellations.
Instead they listen,
search the smeared sleet
for sudden rescue.

Stranded in Shipley
shivering, they fear
they are snowtrapped
in a time warp:
public transport has
plunged into a black hole,
Christmas will never arrive,
the blizzard endless.

Benjamin Ferrand's Folly 1796

'The fast lock'd tower where ivy loves to creep,
Seems like the remains of some old Castle Keep'   Robert Carrick Wildon 1850

Ferrand built a ruin on his land,
a folly on a hill where he could stand
inside the doorway arch to contemplate
the fields and woods and mills of his estate.

He thought a castle with its broken tower,
nestling in a sylvan shaded bower,
couldn't fail to snare a Bingley lass
but this seduction plan proved somewhat crass.

No-one wanted walls without a roof,
a building that was far from weatherproof.
And as for meeting there to court and kiss,
the folly was too cold an edifice.

Poor Ferrand had to wander on his own
and wonder if each ivy-covered stone
should be rebuilt into a hidden grotto,
daubed with some romantic, hopeful motto.

Sad Ferrand died before this cunning plan
could be enacted for the lonely man.
He left no heir, no edict in his will
and so the ruin stayed and stands there still.

Now the walls are sprayed in blue and green
and more than kisses take place at the scene.
The earth is scorched from bonfires lit at night
and litter blows around the woodland site.

Yet something of romance remains today
in Ferrand's Folly, tumbling down and grey.
We're pleased to see his Gothic monument
that speaks to us of pride and sentiment.

Flamborough Head

Flutterfast wings brush the cliff, feet poised to
land on crumbling ledges. Razorbills, gannets,
auks and gulls screech and jostle for position
muscling in to nest and breed on the rock,
beaks open, they stretch necks, clamouring
ownership. We lift binoculars and focus,
ranging through the layers of birds. We see
offspring, white powderpuffs, huddling
under inadequate shelter. Careless
guillemots leave their pyriform eggs
high on shelves, rolling in the wind.

Hovering above the backcombed waves
eager eyes scan for fishflash scales,
avian feathered missile bodies
dive into restless crests of salt water.

Sir Incognito

The tap of your stick
alerts me. You swivel right,
walking with purpose.

Dark glasses disguise,
calf-length boots and winter coat.
Protective armour.

You look up to find
me, waiting at the window.
We wave, smile and nod.

Who and what are you,
my new old friend of five weeks?
You spell out eighty.

I mime disbelief.
The years have not compressed you,
your calm dignity.

Sir Incognito,
I salute you as I rise
from my writing desk.

We both will survive
on unexpected greetings
filling the absence.

While my hair grows grey
uncut, you pace the weeks, months.
We both mark time's tread.

Visitors

Iron kisses under our feet,
sculptured mud in the estuary.
Low tide. A redshank scutters
at the shoreline, dips her beak
again, again, shakes her head.

We like expeditions. Day trips
to different skies, wet horizons
instead of hills before we head
back, keys ready at the door.
Unlike the Kurdish couple

trapped in January, in Hull,
taking selfies to send home.
Her name translates as falling snow.
We hope this port gives sanctuary
under the gaze of Wilberforce.

We watch the Humber swell and rise,
the winter sun retreat behind
The Deep's prow. Whale song echoes
through the streets on wind-drift waves
from Spurn Point. It's time to go.

Nephology

unswept curls of hair   on blue
skids of crystal rain   skystreaked
thin   pauses   smeared punctuation

dragon's breath in
billowed towers
the pencilled puff
on a white page
dissolved
by evening

blurred in winter's
opaque air
collage of greys
stuck and stacked
hilltangled horizon

Haworth Hills

I dreamed last night of Haworth hills,
misty moors and damp days past,
trudging pattens on the cobbles,
Emily breathing hard and fast.

I saw their rooms, the tiny books,
Branwell's painting, creased and brown,
a battered trunk, a Scarborough grave,
lives of passion, all cut down.

I watched the father find his stick,
place his nightcap on his head,
stiffly kneel to say his prayers,
cursing God he was not dead.

Today the Brontës sell as soap
and broken biscuits by the pound.
Thousands come to walk the moors
worshipping the hallowed ground.

The air is clean, the drains are clear,
the deathly coughs are buried deep.
The Brontës have been sanitised,
their untold stories put to sleep.

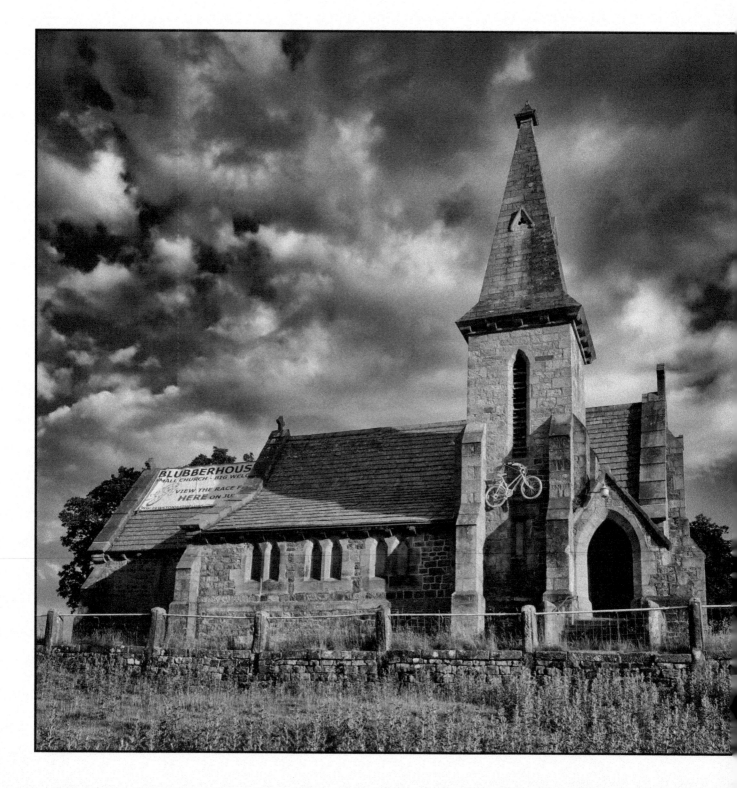

Tour de France, Blubberhouses

Let us hail the yellow bike on high:
its pumped-up tyres, the frame a summer bloom.

Let us pour on oil, anoint the gears,
praise the sleek design of crank and chain.

Let us sing of soaring through the air
above the Yorkshire hills and dry stone walls.

Let us raise our sights, our hopes and hearts
as grey clouds disappear above the spire.

Let us glory in the wise and bold
who blessed this church with flying golden wheels.

Resignation

I know what you're all thinking and saying behind my back:
he shouldn't have to shop for his own tinsel, beard and sack.
And why is he encumbered with an overfilled trolley
when he should be on a sleigh looking fat and pink and jolly?

The reason that I'm scowling and not full of Christmas cheer
is due to recent emails about budget cuts this year.
I've had to sack the reindeer, say goodbye to all my elves.
It's me who's sorting orders and refilling empty shelves.

They've sent these scruffy mutts, not Rudolph and his mates.
My salary's been frozen, despite its measly rates.
My many skills aren't valued, nor my overtime.
And now I'm bagging dog poo. It's all a bloody crime.

I know it could be worse. I might be on the street
like that hooded figure there with the blanket and wet feet.
I've bought myself some goodies - brandy, a Yule log -
survival tools to see me through this festive, dismal slog.

And then I will resign, maybe trundle to the coast
where I will bin this get-up, become a Christmas ghost.
I've had my fill of jollity and all that bloody waste
of money spent on crappy gifts of even crappier taste.

I'll take up taxidermy, employ a smart housekeeper
to help with culling pets - my own Santa's Little Reaper -
who'll find the mutts and moggies for me to strip and stuff.
Goodbye to Ho Ho Ho, the smelly kids. I've had enough.

What I Want

I know it's a horse,
                of course it's a horse,
                                cantering under the tree,

but in my mind's eye
                it's winged and can fly
                                up to the clouds, wild and free.

The sheep pay no heed
                to this galloping steed
                                as they graze on luxurious grass.
They hear the sound
                of hooves on the ground
                                knowing the thunder will pass.

And late in the night
                in the dim-dusk light
                                a horn appears on its head,
a proud unicorn
                struts there until dawn
                                when skies turn from pink to red.

I know it's a horse
                a beast of a horse
                                dappled in dove-white and grey,
but I see a stud
                of mythical blood,
                                enjoying a summer's day.

Bouquet

Poor Ophelia with her floral gifts.
Pansies never eased her heart or cheered.
Forget the rosemary, columbine and rue,
the daisies and the fennel's feathered leaves.
By the river, far from sniffing dogs
I'll pick white stars of garlic growing wild
and in the hills I'll find the nutty scent
of gorse, the yellow tongues among its thorns.
I'll gather cotton grass, the tufts that rise
from swamps to dip and dance in gusts of wind.
My garland will have barley and sea thrift,
stems of pink and purple Yorkshire fog.
I'll give my lover flora from our walks
in sprinkled woods, on moors, on salt-licked cliffs.

ALSO ELLEN LOWE, WHO DIED JANY 8TH
JANY 3RD 1875, AGED 15 YEARS.
MARTHA ELIZABETH HOWELL WH...
30...74 AGED 62 YEARS,
HANNAH ARMISTEAD, WHO DI...
27 1874...
PHILIP...

IN
MEMORY OF
...OTT, WHO DIED MAY 9TH 1886,
...ED 53 YEARS.
...SON, WHO DIED MAY 8TH 1886,
...ED 63 YEARS.
...ITH, WHO DIED MAY 9TH 1886,
...ED 40 YEARS.
...HURST, WHO DIED MAY ... 1886,
...ED 76 YEARS.
...WICK, WHO DIED MAY 16TH 1886,
...24 YEARS.
...DIED MAY 17TH 1886,
...41 YEARS.

IN
MEMORY
...SWAN PARKER, WHO DI...
18...AGED 58
EMMA LETE..., WHO DIED SE...
AGED 81 YEA...
MARY J. TURNER, WHO DIED...
AGED 53 YEA...
GEORGE WHITHAM, WHO DIED...
AGED 7... YEAR...
THOMAS BULMER, WHO DIED...
AGED 7... YEAR...
MARY PICKARD, WHO DIED SE...
AGED 54 YEAR...
JANE ALDERSON, WHO DIED...

Cemetery

We don't know how to talk of the dead,
the families below our feet
sharing graves with strangers.

We kick leaves, ash and beech,
read broken text of broken lives.
Spinster, fettler, bobbin doffer,
MP, linen draper, circus owner, wife.
The stillborn thousands.

This landscaped field is too small
and shallow. We wonder how
they bore it, bear it.

The Naming of Stones

Petrified beings map the moor:
the Twelve Apostles, the Cow and Calf,
the Lanshaw Lad who's never embraced
the Lanshaw Lass across the Delves.

I dip a finger in Weary Stone's cups,
spill the rain from hollowed pools.
The pockmarked rock was worked and scored
millennia ago. We search online

for sketches of the Badger, Neb
and Pepperpot, their rings and rungs,
the crosses with their curling arms
engraved in grit. I don't care

to speculate their role or meaning.
We part the fronds of damp bracken
unsure what we'll find beneath:
the petroglyphs of ancient art

or recent scrawls of names and dates,
hearts like bruises on the rock
exposed to sky, licked by weather,
framed in greens of lichen, moss.

West Riding Pauper Lunatic Asylum

Is this home? I forget.
Stains on green and brown walls
are clouds above my bed.

I watch the ward canary fly
from its cage towards the light.
Sometimes it grips its perch,
stays within the bars.

Sometimes I prefer the dim
inside, the dull calm.

They say it might be good for us
to have fresh air, to weed and rake
the flower beds and walk
the grounds as if we're free.

Marshall tried to hang himself.
The gaslight bracket broke.
Lavatory chains can't be looped
into a noose or knot.

We are watched over,
overseen.

Did I mention the orchestra?
Music made from lunatic strings,
brass and drums, we beat
the wildest rhythms, dance
our madness in and out
with stamping feet and whirl
the staff about until they beg
to be released from jigs and reels.

I think that this is home.

A garden for nesting birds,
the greenest grass,
the smiling face of a clock.

Your Kissing Gate

is missing
her other half.

Curved arms hold
damp air. She waits in rust and tufts
of grass to be repaired, regain
the swinging arc and kiss of metal
lips, the tremble of the fence
when walkers squeeze themselves
against her bars and stop midway,
honouring her moniker.

Your other half
is missing

your kissing.

Harness

I used to watch you fall
through the earth's cracked lid
into caverns that could swallow cathedrals.

You wanted me to applaud
your skill in clipping carabiners,
in rappelling the rope while you spun,

descending in jolts, headlamp
a dim flicker on the limestone walls
wet with Fell Beck's flow.

Now, in Guatemala,
you scramble up San Pedro, slide
on a path of lava, matt black in the sun.

Days later we Skype. Your beard is
shocking. I feel my grip loosen,
try not to tug. I remember you

skinny and laughing on a thread
in Gaping Gill, me at the rim, seeing
you vanish into Hades.

Engagement

I do.

Your threads hold me, pull me into
               your worsted weave. I hear
               your heart in the treadle-beat,
calling me, wooing me.

I stretch my arms across your frame's
               embrace, touch my bridal dress
               of wool, teased and spun on bobbins
that feed your hungry clatter.

Skeins of silk twist light within
               its length. I measure your devotion
               with my hands: my palms' span,
the inches of my thumbs.

Salts Mill beside the Aire will be
               our church, the weir our witness.
               I'll wear your ring of yarn, pledge
myself to you, my loom, my love.

I do.

Where not to be

In the Cheese Press crawling along
black tunnels, trickling water
loud, persistent,
darkness thick as hessian
in front of our eyes,
a dank smell of wet rock.

We rely on helmets,
headlamps blinking on and off
like a dragon's eye.
Our bones vibrate when a train
crosses Ribblehead Viaduct
and we breathe again,
grateful it's not
the roar of a flood
that could flush us out
like drowned ants.

HALL ¾ ml.
RESERVOIR 1ml.
PONDEN KIRK ½ ml.
步道 STANBURY 2½ ml.
Millennium Way
Circular Walk
9

Footpath
歩道

Pilgrims from Japan
take Brontë footsteps over
moorland, worn stone stiles.
The sisters' ghosts follow them,
whisper stories in the wind.

Hawthorn

I'm Whitethorn, Quickthorn, Fairy Tree, May,
footrooted in the limestone grykes, I grow
where others weaken in the windblast blow.

My coat is barkknot weave of brown and grey.
I dance with gales, embrace the falling snow
while bedrock keeps me anchored deep below.

When I wear my budburst leaves, it's Spring.
I thrive and swell with blossoms sweet and white
as songstretched days are drenched in summer light.

My visitors are hundreds on the wing.
My thornsharp arms protect my modest height,
shelter nesting birds from hawk or kite.

In winter my stark branches stroke the sky,
I offer ruby haws to those that fly.
My lone thorn seeds are spread and multiply.

Swinner Gill

I'm walking on a trail above the gill
a grassgroove tipping down towards the edge
I take rainrunnelled steps along the slope
I will not fall I haven't finished yet

The grassgroove tips towards the sodden edge
I hold the rock slipdripping in the damp
I will not fall I haven't started yet
the path is sheep track slither not a path

I grab the rock slipdripping in the wet
water spills across the packhorse bridge
the path is sheep track slide no path in sight
it's not a shower more a downpour gush

water spills across the packhorse bridge
I take rainrunnelled steps along the mud
it's not a shower, more a downpour rush
I'm hanging on to you above the gill

Worship

Our cathedrals stand
in fields. We share our prayers
with swallows, martins.

Shifting skies invade
the roof. Walls tumble, slates slip.
Meadows swallow stone.

We lay offerings
of melancholy thistle.
Birdsong hymns ascend.

Walking away

from you. I'm instructed
to turn my back,
follow the uphill path
until I'm an outline
on the horizon
cushioned in clouds.

You crouch for angles,
line up light
to frame my figure
hugged in her coat
before I'm recalled.

I retrace flagstones
glazed with frost,
stop you checking
every shot. Look at me.
Not my image.
I'm here. Freezing.

10-11 Offcumdens

Bob: There wasn't much discussion needed to settle on this photograph for the title poem. It captures that combination of the wild and the tamed which is so characteristic of the Yorkshire Dales, paths leading through walled pastures to the high moors. This is the landscape that I fell in love with when I first came to Yorkshire, as a student, to go potholing. One morning, bruised and sore, my wetsuit in tatters, I chose to spend the day walking instead of caving. I've never looked back. The photograph is a view of the head of Littondale, shot from the track that leads from the village of Halton Gill over the top of Horse Head and down to Yockenthwaite in Langstrothdale. It was taken on a late October afternoon, at a time when the days are rapidly getting shorter and the shadows longer. The summit of Ingleborough can be seen in the far distance. (28/10/2018)

Emma: I have Viking roots, the name Storr meaning big or strong in Old Norse. When I went to Whitby, I discovered several Storr graves in St Mary's Churchyard. I feel I have come home and don't intend to leave. Many Yorkshire villages have Norse names and the term 'wapentake' is apparently of Scandinavian origin. A wapentake is an administrative area, a subdivision of the three Yorkshire Ridings.

12-13 Mirror

Bob: I live near Ilkley Tarn and this photograph was taken from a spot I pass frequently, most often on days of very little wind, looking to find a perfect reflection. There's an inlet to the tarn close by that can disturb the surface. The resident duck population doesn't always oblige by staying out of the way. I've taken many versions of this photograph but the absolute stillness of this particular day was unusual, as were the patterns in the sky. It was one of those moments I savour as a photographer, when all the various elements come together. I remember rushing home in excitement, knowing that I had something special, looking forward to seeing how it would process in black and white. It was a shot that was made to be inverted. (10/1/2018)

Emma: This was one of the first photographs of Bob's that I saw and loved. The reversal of the sky and pond inspired me to write a concrete poem, the words laid out in a visual pattern that echoes the photograph's imagery.

14-15 The Leeds Library

Bob: Founded in 1768, The Leeds Library is the oldest surviving subscription library in the country. Hidden away on Commercial Street behind an unprepossessing entrance, most passers-by don't even register its existence. I was in this category until I finally discovered it a couple of years ago. Walking in from a busy shopping street, its staircase offers a portal into another world and another time. It's now become a kind of second home. I wanted to find a less obvious take on the library's many special spaces and this shot is taken along one of the iron walkways that were a late addition to the New Room (itself an addition dating from 1880), as the library's collection grew rapidly through the 19th century. (19/02/2018)

Emma: The Leeds Library has become our favourite haunt in the centre of Leeds, a place where we often convene to read and to write. Many of the older books with faded covers remain on the shelves unborrowed for years, maybe centuries. My poem is a sonnet, a poetic form devised many centuries ago that seemed an appropriate way to honour this hallowed place. Check out www.theleedslibrary.org.uk

16-17 Busker

Bob: It's ironic that the Reading Room in The Leeds Library, supposedly the quietest of its three public spaces, is the noisiest. Particularly in summer, when its two windows are propped open, music drifts in from the various buskers who perform outside on Commercial Street, a busy pedestrianised route. The quality varies significantly. I encountered Sam Brown, pictured here, on my way to the library one morning and was stopped, spellbound by her music, surrounded by shoppers rushing past. I stayed listening for quite a while, as if being given my own personal concert performance. She uses a loop pedal to lay down a backing track and then plays her songs on top of that. It's right to call them songs because she makes her violin sing with a unique voice. She's studying Jazz at Leeds College of Music. (19/8/2019)

Emma: I remember Bob taking me out of the library to meet Sam after he'd been very impressed by her skill and elegance. My poem is deliberately succinct in an attempt to capture the brief and haunting music that Sam conjured from the violin, the notes travelling along the length of the street.

Hear Sam's music at: https://sambrownviolinist.bandcamp.com

18-19 Wall

Bob: Nowhere in the Dales is the land more intricately and improbably divided by dry stone walls than in Swaledale. This shot was taken from the east side of Swinner Gill on a high level path that can be followed after crossing the River Swale beyond Muker. It continues on past Crackpot Hall (to be seen far left) to Keld. It's an area where lead mining once flourished and it was subsidence from mining activity that led to the farmhouse of Crackpot Hall being evacuated in 1953. (29/9/2020)

Emma: Dry stone walls are always cropping up in my poems because of their interesting shapes, their structure and the way they flow across the Yorkshire landscape. The sonnet form also has structure and has to be built with careful attention to rhythm and stresses.

20-21 St Aidan's, RSPB

Bob: St Aidan's is a nature reserve sited on a former opencast coal mine to the east of Leeds. We turned up on a day of clear blue skies in April. I'm far more of a people watcher than a bird watcher so almost all my photographs were of fellow visitors to the reserve. The process here, when we've been somewhere together, is for me to select my favourite photographs and share them with Emma, to see if anything might germinate. It's very much like planting a seed. It's been fascinating to observe which ones have taken to life and then been able to watch them grow into fully-fledged poems. (21/4/2019)

Emma: St Aidan's was a new and unexpected discovery a few years ago when I was out with a walking group. This reclaimed mining site is now a wetlands haven for many birds, including the rare bittern. Oddball is a leviathan of a walking dragline excavator that dominates the site and provides nesting opportunities for falcons and owls. I was also as interested in the birders and twitchers as in the birds themselves. Check out www.walkingdragline.org

22-23 Letter to Prof Armitage

Emma: I wrote a version of this poem in 2016. The Stanza Stone trail is a 47-mile walking track between Marsden and Ilkley linking six poems by the poet Simon Armitage that were commissioned by the Ilkley Literature Festival in 2010 and carved by Pip Hall. There were rumours of the existence of a seventh Stanza stone. This poem is a piece of doggerel because I like writing light-hearted pieces and teasing the Poet Laureate.

Bob: This was the easiest poem to respond to with a photograph, not least because the Beck Stone, pictured here, is situated only a couple of minutes walk from where I live. I wanted to capture the beck in spate and simply had to wait for a prolonged period of heavy rain. It's never a long wait. (3/9/2020)
More information at www.simonarmitage.com/stanza-stones

24-25 Dancing Girls

Bob: When I was working in Shipley I used to do a lot of street photography around the market square in the centre of town, capturing candid pictures of people going about their lives. These three ladies caught my attention one lunchtime, lost in animated conversation. Alice, on the left, had known Winnie, in the middle, for well over 70 years, from when they first met as young girls working at Salts Mill in Saltaire, just a half mile away. They told me that the machines were so loud it was impossible to hear each other speak. They had their own sign language to communicate. Vera, on the right, is Winnie's elder sister. When this shot was taken, all three ladies were in their late eighties. (17/05/2013)

Emma: When Bob told me that these three women in Shipley had all been mill workers, I was inspired to invent their back stories. I enjoyed imagining that they could slip out of old age and the ugly shoes that older women often have to wear.

26-27 Cycle

Emma: I wrote this poem during the Tour de France in 2014 when the Dales were filled with Yorkshire men and women in Lycra who had fallen in love with their bikes again, or who were inspired by the event to take up cycling. The subtext might be a certain neglect of other people or concerns that require attention, but it is also a celebration of the symbiotic relationship between cyclist and bike.

Bob: Although written before we knew each other, I found this poem spoke to me in a very personal way. The chosen photograph was taken close to the time when the Tour de France came to Yorkshire. I was cycling to work on a brilliantly sunny morning, stopped to take in the view across Baildon Moor, looked down and noticed this image. I feel very at one with my bike and thought this captured the unity of man and machine that Emma expresses in her poem. (14/04/2014)

28-29 Huggate Poetry Bench

Bob: I know the east of the county less well than the north and west and Emma was keen for me to explore the Wolds. In the flat light of an overcast November day, we found ourselves held within the folds of the clouds as much as the folds of the landscape itself. There is a softness to the hills here that is very different to the Dales. (26/11/2020)

Emma: I'd come across the poetry bench some years before. At that time it had a tupperware box with pencil and paper for passing walkers to leave poems inspired by walking The Wolds Way. I revisited the lines I had written then and reworked them into couplets. I liked the fact that the cows were indifferent to our presence, my poetry and Bob's camera.

30-31 Legend

Bob: The Cow and Calf rocks in Ilkley are very well known and attract visitors throughout the year. I encouraged Emma to develop her own take on the legend of the giant Rombald and the creation of this iconic feature of the landscape. This is the view that first greets most people on arrival. Living nearby, I've taken hundreds of pictures, from every possible angle, but classic felt the way to go here. (26/2/2020)

Emma: The legend of how the Cow and Calf rocks became separated interested me. It involves a rowing couple who both came to grief and ended up dividing a mother from her offspring. I wanted to tell the story as briefly as possible and emphasise the permanent damage caused.

32-33 Cinematic

Bob: There's not a lot to be said about the photograph itself. The cinema offers a throwback to a time when cinemas were picture houses. The Hyde Park Picture House in Headingley is an iconic feature of Leeds. As you step through the doors, it feels as if you are entering a bygone era. We saw the film *Capernaum* here as part of the Leeds International Film Festival. (8/11/2018)

Emma: We both agreed that this was an extraordinary film and we remained deeply affected as we walked away from the cinema that evening. The poem was prompted by many emotions: horror at the poverty and desperation of street children and refugees in Lebanon and also guilt about the privileged and sheltered lives we currently lead.

34-35 Upright Motives

Bob: It was a bright September day for my first ever visit to the Yorkshire Sculpture Park. Henry Moore's *Upright Motives*, sited not far from the main entrance, is one of the first pieces you are likely to come across. We might not have stopped to look so closely at this work if it hadn't been for Mick being so diligent in cleaning each totem. As I took this photograph, focussing on the composition, I was unaware of who I'd framed in the shot. It was only later that we recognised the poet, Ian McMillan, walking around with his grandson. By an even stranger coincidence, when Emma introduced herself as a fellow poet, he recognised her name from having just reviewed her recently published pamphlet, *Heart Murmur* for *The North* poetry magazine. It was a lovely moment of serendipity. (22/9/2020)

Emma: Neither of us had realised that washing the sculptures and removing bird droppings from them takes place regularly. It was a delight to meet and chat to Mick Johnson and Ian McMillan. Bob captured both encounters in this photo and I have tried to do the same in a sequence of haiku. Check out www.ysp.org.uk

36-37 Dog Days

Bob: Working in Shipley over a number of years, I didn't venture into the centre of town for a long time. I tended to take lunch at my desk, barely taking a break. But then, encouraged by a virtual friend from Portland, Oregon, who was capturing life on one of her local streets, I started taking candid street photographs around the market and getting in conversation with the local people. I took time to stop and listen to their stories and lunch hour soon became the highlight of my day. Working in the abstract world of computer software, that short trip into town provided a much-needed shot of perspective. The visual stories told by my street photographs are open to interpretation. I left it to Emma to choose one and create her own.

Emma: I loved the detail of this photograph. Despite not seeing the face of the woman in this shot, I could imagine her life in which this Shih Tzu played an important role. That led to me wanting to write a poem in the voice of the dog and reverse the idea of 'walkies'.

38-39 Brocken Spectre

Bob: Brocken Spectres are generally regarded as a mountain phenomenon and only rarely seen. I have mountain loving friends who've never seen one in a lifetime of hillwalking. The weather has to be just right. They appear when the sun shines from behind you when standing on a ridge looking down upon a layer of cloud or fog in misty conditions. The light is scattered to form a circular rainbow around the shadow of your head, called a glory. Ilkley Moor happens to be a spectre hotspot. There are usually three or four days each year when the right conditions occur. Luckily I have a radar that alerts me to the possibility of seeing one, waking me up to get outside with an urgency that denies me having a cup of tea first, before the fog burns off or dissipates. There's only ever a narrow window of opportunity and you have to be in exactly the right place at exactly the right time. Local knowledge is very useful. (31/1/2019)

Emma: I had never heard of this phenomenon before Bob explained the unusual weather conditions that can lead to its appearance. Millions of years ago Ilkley Moor was covered by ocean and I could imagine ships navigating a sea of mist.

40-41 Grand Départ – Côte de Cray

Bob: As a lifelong cyclist and keen follower of the Tour de France, it was beyond my wildest dreams when Yorkshire won the right to hold the Grand Départ in 2014. The best cyclists in the world were going to be riding on my local roads, the greatest sporting spectacle in the world coming to my own backyard. The weather gods played their part, delivering a sunny day of perfect visibility, showcasing the Yorkshire landscape at its very best. I rode out from Ilkley, following the route of this opening stage of the race, thousands of spectators already there watching and cheering us amateurs on, several hours before the pros were due to pass by. I found a spot to watch at Kidstones, close to the summit of the climb from Cray over into Bishopdale. (5/7/2014)

Emma: The cyclists were so close to each other that they seemed like one huge organic whole, a breathing mass of animal power surging past the crowd within touching distance. Their helmets resembled large insect eyes and the pounding legs could have belonged to a giant centipede.

42-43 Eighteen Miles

Emma: Salts Mill was one of the largest textile mills in Europe in the mid-nineteenth century and could produce eighteen miles of cloth in one day. Sir Titus Salt was apparently a benign employer and looked after his staff much better than many other mill owners. There's an affinity between a loom and a harp for me, between woven material and a musical score.

Bob: I used to walk along this stretch of canal on a daily basis, from the station at Shipley to where I worked, an office beside the canal that was situated underneath the leftmost, the nearest, of the three chimneys you can see in this image. The rightmost one, by far the tallest, belongs to Salts Mill at Saltaire. Looking for a photograph to accompany Emma's poem, this one jumped out at me as the perfect shot, with all the right associations. The Leeds-Liverpool Canal was central to all the industry that once thrived here. (1/12/2011)

44-45   Exposure

Emma: Bob is the only person I know who adores fog for the very good reasons he has outlined above in his notes on the Brocken Spectre. I wrote this poem for him a few months after we had met. It was published in the bi-annual poetry magazine *Pennine Platform*, Issue 87, 2020.

Bob: Waking up to the sight of fog out of the window gets me out of bed like a child on Christmas morning. I never know what photographic opportunities are going to be presented, if any at all. I'm regularly disappointed, climbing up to the top of Ilkley Moor through thick mist and failing to emerge into the clear skies that I know are above. There is often a hint of blue overhead, suggesting that the surface of the inversion layer is tantalisingly close. It's called an inversion because a layer of warmer air is acting as a lid on the mist below, holding it in place. In winter it can stay locked in the valley all day. Normally, it burns off as the sun rises or it gets disturbed by a freshening wind. The mist rolls in and out like a tide. I head for the areas of pine woodland that fringe the moorland in this tidal zone, looking for sunbursts through the trees. They can appear and be gone again in a matter of seconds. (10/4/2016)

46-47   Shelter

Bob: While working in Shipley I developed a great affection for the sturdily built bus shelters that line one side of the market square. Each one seemed to have its own character as determined by the personalities of the people waiting. I consistently found that some shelters were friendlier than others, the inhabitants more likely to engage with me and offer an opportunity to take photographs. I would tend to gravitate towards those, each a little microcosm of the local communities being served by that particular bus route. This one was always my favourite. (2/3/2016)

Emma: When I saw this photo, I was worried that the bus might never arrive. I wanted to transport these poor cold people to another planet before they were frozen in time and weather forever.

48-49   Benjamin Ferrand's Folly 1796

Bob: As a photographer, I'm not alone in holding a fascination for decay and dereliction. Emma led a walk from Saltaire up through Cottingley Woods, keeping quiet about this artificially dilapidated structure so that I was wonderfully unprepared for its unexpected appearance in the forest. The Folly was built to be admired on the skyline from the valley below. The modern plantation of trees now blocks that view but being hidden in the woods makes it even more of a folly, as well as a place of romance and imagination.

Emma: The Folly is a delightful structure on the St Ives estate near Bingley. I used rhyme in this poem because it seemed to suit the old fashioned sentiment and topic. The quote from Robert Carrick Wildon is from a long poem he wrote in 1850 titled *Lines suggested while sitting at the Ruins*.

50-51   Flamborough Head

Bob: Flamborough Head, on the east coast of Yorkshire between Filey and Bridlington, hosts a large seabird colony. I don't aspire to wildlife photography, lacking possession of both the patience and the equipment required to take good pictures. Walking along at the edge of the cliffs, it was extraordinary to observe the comings and goings of the seabirds, as well as those photographers we found stationed by their tripods, huge lenses focussed on the puffins. Everyone, it seems, loves a puffin. I prefer the less showy kittiwakes, seen here nesting on the chalk cliffs. The chicks are protected from predators but they clearly live a precarious existence before they find their wings. In winter, these birds spend their months out at sea, only returning in the summer to breed, perhaps even returning to the same vertiginous perch. (26/6/2020)

Emma: We had a delightful summer walk on the cliffs at Flamborough during peak breeding season for seabirds. I chose to do an acrostic poem as a challenge. I wonder how many people noticed this?

52-53   Sir Incognito

Emma: The first lockdown due to the Covid pandemic led to me spending a lot of time at my desk in the bay window of my first floor bedroom. One of the people I noticed was a man who walked down my street at more or less the same time every morning. Often he would look up and we got in the habit of waving at each other. I was inspired to write a series of haiku about him before we met. We have become good friends since that chance encounter. *Sir Incognito* was published in the Wharfedale Poets Anthology *On the Other Side* (Ings Poetry, 2020).

Bob: Unusually for me, this is a staged photograph, which I hope can be forgiven as it simply wasn't possible to capture the moment during lockdown. I was relayed the story of Sir Incognito over the phone. It was lovely, once restrictions eased in the summer, to meet Malcolm and chat over a cup of coffee. (17/6/2021)

54-55   Visitors

Bob: It was Emma who organised a trip to Hull, simply telling me to meet her at Leeds station to catch a train—somewhere. She'd been surprised to find out, a few weeks before, that I'd never visited a city of which she was a great fan. I was fascinated by the juxtaposition of old and new, particularly here where the rusting iron of an old jetty is contrasted with the clean lines of The Deep, the city's striking aquarium, a centre for marine research and conservation. (8/1/2019)

Emma: On this day trip to Hull in winter we met a young couple from Kurdistan. Their story made us think about our own good fortune in contrast to the difficulties faced by thousands of immigrants and refugees who end up in the UK, often in deprived areas on the coast.

56-57   Nephology

Emma: I wrote this concrete poem as an exercise during a poetry course with The Poetry School, tutored by Seán Hewitt. Bob loves cloud formations and dramatic skies are a constant feature in his photos.

Bob: As a landscape photographer I am forever watching the clouds. Rarely going out to take a specific shot, my photographs invariably arrive as a result of being in the right place at the right time, which happened to be my bedroom on this occasion. The shot was taken through the window. I'd only just got back from being out on the moor for a few hours, watching the formation of some cumulonimbus monsters and managing to avoid getting soaked. This was the biggest of them all. Yorkshire doesn't have a monopoly on clouds, of course, but I've always felt closer to them here. (16/6/2020)

58-59   Haworth Hills

Emma: One of our first expeditions together in 2018 was to Haworth. I have a print of Bob's photograph on my wall to remind me of the lovely couple of days we spent walking on the moors. I was giving a talk for the Brontë Parsonage titled 'Drink, Disease and Death' describing some of the causes of the very high mortality rate in Haworth in the 19th-century. Life expectancy was between 18 and 25 years according to the Babbage Report of 1850. All six of the Brontë children died prematurely, two in childhood and four in early adulthood. Their father, the Reverend Patrick Brontë, survived into his eighties, having endured the loss of his wife and then all his children. I wrote the poem many years ago after visiting the Brontë Parsonage and reading about the unhealthy and unsanitary living conditions. 'Pattens' were overshoes usually made of wood with a thick heel. They protected the wearer from the mud and effluent in the streets and kept the inner shoe clean.

Bob: Walking the hills around Haworth, especially when taking the well-worn track to Top Withens, invariably along with many other visitors, it's hard not to feel that the wild moors of Wuthering Heights have been tamed and sanitised for modern consumption. I decided upon a photograph that avoids any bleakness, the sun catching the hills beyond, the solitary tree resonating with the melancholy tone of Emma's poem. (28/04/2018)

60-61 Tour de France, Blubberhouses

Bob: When the Tour de France came to Yorkshire, yellow bikes started popping up all over the county. They were to be seen sitting in hedges, locked to gates, hoisted upon roofs. They became a kind of physical meme. People found unused bikes, spray-painted them yellow, and exhibited them for passers-by to see. It was a remarkable show of solidarity from a county that was already becoming known for its rich cycling culture. Seven years on, many of these yellow bikes are still to be seen in place, a lasting celebration of two exceptional days in the county's history. The sun shone and never have more people around the world been able to witness the beauty of the Yorkshire landscape. This particular bike, suspended on the tower of St Andrew's Church, Blubberhouses, has since been removed, although it took quite a while. (23/6/2014)

Emma: It was pleasing that even the local church was keen to join in the celebrations and put a yellow bicycle on its tower. I wrote a praise song to reflect the reverence that the Tour de France evoked in Yorkshire and the religious fervour of its followers.

62-63 Resignation

Bob: This shot was taken in the entrance way of The Leeds Library, just as I was leaving on a very grey and wet morning. I saw this Santa approaching and knew right away that there was a photograph to be taken. Christmas is not my favourite time of year and this image captures a sense of its sadder side. This is taken on Commercial Street. (21/12/2018)

Emma: I've always felt sorry for Father Christmas. He has an impossible and demanding job. Bob's photo conveyed a certain reluctance on the part of this man to look jolly and inspired these rhyming lines.

64-65 What I Want

Bob: This shot was taken on a particularly favourite cycle route that I ride often from Ilkley. It's a circuit out to Malham that when ridden anticlockwise brings you back on the little lane from Winterburn to Hetton. It was here I saw this free-spirited grey, galloping around a field containing a magnificent ash tree. It was only a matter of seconds before the sun came out and the horse passed by the tree in the perfect place. (31/8/2014)

Emma: The photo of the horse in motion under the splendid tree suggested a mythical beast. I tried to capture the movement of the horse using rhyme, rhythm and space between dropped lines.

66-67 Bouquet

Emma: This sonnet celebrates common plants rather than flowers and I liked the idea of gathering them for Bob after we had seen many of them growing locally. The smell of wild garlic permeates the air in late spring. I was delighted to find that one of the most attractive grasses, with a purplish-pink hue, is known as Yorkshire fog. Bog cotton (cottongrass) looks like cotton wool blowing in the wind high on the moors.

Bob: Appearing towards the end of May and usually lasting through June, I look forward to the displays of cottongrass as much as the flowering of the heather later in the summer, when huge swathes of the moor get painted purple. The bog cotton provides for a less ostentatious display, one far more amenable to black and white photography. As a sedge rather than a grass, and distinctly not cotton, its common names are misnomers but perfectly appropriate. Displays vary greatly from year to year depending on how much moisture there is in the ground. It thrives in areas of boggy moorland. Watching the tufts blowing in the wind, it's impossible not to marvel at nature's ingenuity when it comes to pollination. (27/5/2017)

68-69   Cemetery

Bob: I'd previously only known St George's Field as somewhere quiet to lay on the grass and read a book of a summer lunchtime. Revisiting with Emma, I learned more about its history and the fact that the Burial Registers have been digitised and are searchable online at the Special Collections Library at the University of Leeds. Many of the headstones were controversially removed in 1968 when the cemetery was landscaped to the green space it is today. The photograph is of a detail of the closely-packed flat stone tablets that have been left in one corner, hinting at the density of the burials. I've always been fascinated by gravestones. Those short inscriptions connect us to a whole life lived centuries ago, often cut tragically short but sometimes enduring into a surprisingly old age. A quick search on one of the names, Thomas Bulmer, revealed that he died of consumption at the age of 20. He was a coach-maker by profession. In the light of that little bit of knowledge, he suddenly becomes a real person and his death so much more poignant. (31/07/2018)

Emma: The Leeds Cemetery in St George's Field at the University of Leeds has over 97,000 burials. The Burial Registers record cause of death, employment, age and date. Nearly half of all the burials are children under the age of 9 years. It is difficult to imagine how people in the past coped with frequent family deaths, often of the very young. I often take medical students to the cemetery when teaching about diseases of the past, particularly those affecting the children of the poor, whose mortality rates were appallingly high during the Industrial Revolution. My poem tries to convey the pain of loss, then and now.

70-71   The Naming of Stones

Emma: Ilkley Moor has many named stones, some of which have Neolithic carvings of curly crosses, parallel lines and cup and ring marks. The significance of these is unknown but they were described and drawn in great detail by 19th-century historians and archaeologists. There's also a lot of graffiti from the Victorian era as well as more recent designs and etchings of initials and hearts with dates. Three of the six Stanza Stones, carved with poems on the theme of water by Simon Armitage, can be found around Ilkley Moor: the Puddle Stone, the Dew Stone and the Beck Stone.

Bob: Although there were a plethora of options when it came to picking this photograph of the Hanging Stone for Emma's poem, it wasn't a difficult choice to make. The stone sits directly above where I live and alongside the quarry that provided the gritstone for Ilkley's grand houses. This flat slab of rock was saved (mostly) from the quarrying when its historical significance was recognised, just in time. I sometimes sit up here and ponder the meaning of the cup and ring markings on these rocks. I've waited for the sun to set on the longest day and watched it disappear behind the moor above Cracoe in a position aligned with two of the circular cups. This particular shot was taken close to the time of the winter solstice. You can imagine the line of the outer ring being a representation of the profile of the moor beyond, the placing of the cups indicating when the shortest day is reached. (30/12/2016)

72-73   West Riding Pauper Lunatic Asylum

Emma: The asylum was built in 1888 in Menston, near Leeds and was renamed High Royds Hospital in 1963. It was a large institution that at one time had its own bakers, butchers, dairy, dispensary and linked railway. Some of the information I used to write this poem came from reading the memories of FE Rogers who used to work there. While asylums are generally viewed negatively, many offered a safe and caring environment for the mentally disturbed and organised regular entertainment to cheer up the patients and staff.

Bob: High Royds is not easy to photograph. Its sprawling complex of Victorian buildings is now an upmarket housing development. An initial wander around the site wasn't particularly successful and it was only months later, when I was out cycling, descending from the Chevin, that this image presented itself. It was there and gone in a flash, seen through a gap in the hedgerow. It's the only view I've ever found that's free of any modern clutter and the only photograph I've ever taken that comes close to capturing the former asylum's grandiosity. It was worth the price of having to do battle with the thorns and nettles in order to find the right angle. (10/6/2021) Check out www.highroydshospital.com.

74-75 Your Kissing Gate

Bob: This shot was taken on a grey autumnal day on the way home from a trip to Swaledale with Emma, stopping off for a walk in Wensleydale. The kissing gate is to be found on a footpath that joins the picturesque villages of Worton and Askrigg after it crosses some meadows and the disused railway line, just as the path starts to climb above the floodplain to the north of the River Ure. It's never possible to predict whether an image is going to work or not, but I had a hunch this might elicit a poetic response from Emma. (2/10/2020)

Emma: This lonely remnant of a kissing gate inspired the poem which also relates to the restrictions imposed on many people during the 2020 Covid pandemic and the repeated lockdowns.

76-77 Harness

Emma: I have never been down Gaping Gill, the huge limestone cave near the village of Clapham in North Yorkshire, but the dangers of caving provided a good metaphor for the difficulties of letting go of an adult child. This poem was published in the bi-annual poetry magazine *Pennine Platform*, Issue 86, 2019.

Bob: I have a long history with Gaping Gill. It's the largest underground chamber in the country and is often quoted as being expansive enough to house a cathedral. I first got dropped down here during my caving adventures in Yorkshire as a student. We spent many hours exploring the wider network of passages and exiting somewhere else altogether (there are a number of entrances to the system). Two local clubs hold winch meets each year around the bank holidays at the end of May (Bradford Pothole Club) and at the end of August (Craven Pothole Club), where anyone can don a hard hat and pay to be lowered down. Health and Safety determines that people definitely get lowered now, sedately, as opposed to dropped under gravity with a late application of the brakes, which is how I remember my first descent. There is lots of water spraying around at the bottom, as well as very little light, so as far as the photograph was concerned, it was a matter of simply pointing and hoping for the best. I was pleased to see the result. (10/8/2018)

78-79 Engagement

Emma: I wrote this poem during a poetry workshop with Carol Ann Duffy at the National Writing Centre of Wales at Ty Newydd in 2018. We had to imagine forming a relationship with an inanimate object. This poem won 3rd prize in the Saltaire Festival Poetry competition of 2019.

Bob: I saw this poem as something of a celebration of Yorkshire's industrial past and the extraordinary engineering that put the county, with its rivers and canals, and then its coal, at the centre of the Industrial Revolution. Armley Mills, once the world's largest woollen mill, is now home to Leeds Industrial Museum. It was closed during the first Covid lockdown and we had to wait for it to reopen before we could visit and start looking around the machinery halls for the right image. The looms are marvels of cast-iron ingenuity. (21/10/2020) Check out http://www.industrialmuseum.leeds.gov.uk

80-81 Where Not To Be

Emma: Many years ago I went caving with my children in the underground passages of Long Churn Cave, not far from Ribblehead Viaduct. I remember the anxiety about flash floods or getting stuck in the narrow passage of the Cheese Press, particularly as there had been a recent tragedy when two schoolchildren had drowned during a gorge walk not far away.

Bob: To accompany Emma's poem I wanted to take a less obvious approach, hinting at the limestone terrain that's riddled underneath with holes and passages, the result of rain falling on the hard gritstone peaks and running off to disappear into the permeable limestone. The water turns acidic and has dissolved the rock over millions of years, exploiting joints and bedding planes. Trains pass over on their way from Settle to Carlisle, the passengers oblivious to Yorkshire's secret and spectacular underground landscape. (13/9/2020)

82-83   Footpath

Emma: This poem is written in the form of a Japanese tanka, similar to a haiku but slightly longer. It is usually composed of five lines with a syllable count distribution of 5/7/5/7/7. Haworth is a popular tourist destination for Japanese devotees of the Brontës' novels and the footpath signs on the moors are bilingual.

Bob: This photograph was taken in response to an idea for a possible poem, which emerged spontaneously when we came across this signpost. I loved the incongruity. (31/8/2020)

84-85   Hawthorn

Bob: I love solitary trees, especially in winter when they present their naked skeletons. Each one has a distinct personality characterised by its shape and setting. I particularly love the wild hawthorns of the Dales, often seen sprouting out from the limestone escarpments or pavements, almost as if they are rooted in the rock itself. The grykes offer the seedlings a protected environment at the start of their life. This particular tree is situated at Nab End, above Cowside Beck and below the narrow road that runs from Arncliffe out over Malham Moor. (2/3/2013)

Emma: Many of the limestone ridges in the Dales have single hawthorn trees that have taken root. I researched some of the folklore and ecosystem of the hawthorn before I wrote this poem. The rhyme scheme emerged as I shaped the lines and words.

86-87   Swinner Gill

Bob: What makes the Yorkshire Dales so special for walking and cycling is that the landscape is changing all the time, made possible because its scale is an intimate, very human one. It has serious hills but they're not mountains to climb. It doesn't take long to travel from one valley over into another, the paths finding a way through the limestone outcrops, rocks polished smooth by the footfall of hundreds of years. This is another photograph taken above Swinner Gill, the removal of the horizon accentuating the steepness of the valley. By chance, the very next day we found ourselves on the vertiginous path to be seen in the top half of the photograph. The weather had turned wet and windy by then and the rocks proved to be very slippery in the rain. (29/9/2020)

Emma: My poem is in the form of a pantoum, a poem with four line stanzas in which the second and fourth lines of each stanza repeat as the first and third lines of the next stanza. The repetition emphasised the fear I felt walking along a slippery, narrow and steep slope above a small stream. Bob is more sure-footed and sometimes takes me on very challenging routes. We were heading towards a deserted lead mining site.

88-89   Worship

Emma: Littondale and Swaledale are dotted with large hay barns in adjoining meadows. Many of these are beautifully constructed and seem as worthy of worship as churches or cathedrals.

Bob: I'm forever passing stone barns whilst out walking or cycling in the Dales. It's hard to resist a stop to take pictures of them, even in places where I've already done so several times before. Many are very well preserved. Some have fallen into complete ruin. The best subjects for photography are those that fall between those extremes, where decay has set in to reveal the layers of construction but not to the extent that the integrity of the building has been destroyed. Perhaps it's the suggestion of transformation and transience that makes such structures so appealing to the photographic eye. Perhaps it is also where we find the sense of the sacred that Emma hints at in her poem. (28/10/2018)

90-91   Walking away

Bob: Emma is called upon to be very patient while we're out walking together. I see something in the landscape that I think will make for a good photograph and go running off to find the right spot. Sometimes she has a long wait before I catch up with her again. I often see shapes and textures in the patterns of the clouds, imagining how they are going to look in black and white. I had this shot in my mind's eye as soon as we reached the path near the Cow and Calf on Ilkley Moor, taken well before the idea for the book emerged. (6/10/2018)

Emma: It can get very cold waiting for Bob to take photos and then checking them to make sure he has the shot he's after. This photo was taken in March with frost on the ground in a bitter wind. My devotion to art, and to Bob, was somewhat tested.

Bob Hamilton

is a Londoner who moved to Ilkley in 1988. He has a background in mathematics and spent his working life as a software developer, involving everything from computer games in the 80s to image databases in the 90s—pioneering the first systems for museums to display their photographic archives on screens—to public health systems in the 2000s. Somewhere in the middle of all that coding he took a sabbatical to write a non-fiction book called *Earthdream* (Green Books, 1990), a work of ecophilosophy. With his family having spread its wings, he has found the space to pick up his camera and his pen again, pursuing a number of photography and writing projects. He has won a number of open photography competitions and has had his pictures exhibited nationwide through The Photographic Angle.

Web: www.earthdreamery.co.uk and www.facebyface.org.uk

Emma Storr

is also a Londoner who moved to Leeds in 1993. She has a background in medicine but is now turning her attention to poetry. She completed an MPhil in Writing at the University of South Wales in 2018. Publications include poems in *The Hippocrates Prize Anthologies* of 2016, 2018 and 2020, *Strix* Nos. 2, 3 & 4, *Pennine Platform* Issues 86 & 87 and *Raceme* No.8. Her poems have appeared in the following anthologies: *These Are The Hands* (Fair Acre Press, 2020), *And the Stones Fell Open* (Yaffle Press, 2020), *When All This Is Over* (Calder Valley Poetry, 2020), *On the Other Side* (Ings Poetry, 2020) and *Bloody Amazing* (Dragon Yaffle, 2020). Her debut pamphlet *Heart Murmur* was published by Calder Valley Poetry in 2019 and has a medical theme, based on her work as a GP.

Web: www.emmastorr.co.uk

Acknowledgements

Bob

Many of the photographs reproduced here came about as the result of belonging to a small online photo-journaling community called Blipfoto, a site designed for recording each day with a single photograph and a few words. I aimed to post every day for a year and, like many others, continued for much longer, getting hooked by the daily challenge. I owe thanks to many members of the Blipfoto community but particularly to Andrea Schuh, from whom I inherited my love of the square format.

Sometimes on our joint expeditions around Yorkshire, Emma has seen a photographic opportunity that I might otherwise have missed. I'm indebted to her for pointing these out. I'm also hugely grateful for her patience.

Finally, thanks are due to the Leeds Industrial Museum for permission to use the photograph for *Engagement*, The Leeds Library for permission to use the photograph for *The Leeds Library*, and to the Yorkshire Sculpture Park and the Henry Moore Foundation for permission to use the photograph for *Upright Motives*.

Emma

Several poems in *Offcumdens* have been honed and improved in response to feedback from various writing groups. The Leeds Writers Circle, the Wharfedale Poets, and Antony Dunn's Poetry School seminars have been invaluable in this process. Fellow poets Lydia Kennaway, Carole Bromley and Charlotte Eichler have provided perceptive comments, particularly with attention to the music and rhythm of the words. Bob has been a constant source of encouragement and critical help in his appraisal of each poem.

Engagement won 3rd prize in the Saltaire Festival Poetry competition, 2019.
Harness was published in *Pennine Platform* Issue 86, 2019.
Exposure was published in *Pennine Platform* Issue 87, 2020.
Sir Incognito was published in *On The Other Side, Writing by the Wharfedale Poets*, Ings Poetry, 2020.
A version of *The Leeds Library* was published in The Leeds Library bi-monthly newsletter *Speaks Volumes,* 24 December 2020.
Dancing Girls won 1st prize and *Eighteen Miles* won 2nd prize in the Saltaire Festival Poetry competition, 2021.

Milton Keynes UK
Ingram Content Group UK Ltd.
UKHW050629271124
3179UKWH00023B/214